Huntingdon Area
Middle School IMC
Huntingdon, Pa.

Class No.
599.73

Acc. No.
13684

THE GIRAFFE

BY
CARL R. GREEN
WILLIAM R. SANFORD

EDITED BY
DR. HOWARD SCHROEDER, Ph.D.
Professor in Reading and Language Arts
Dept. of Curriculum and Instruction
Mankato State University

PRODUCED AND DESIGNED BY
BAKER STREET PRODUCTIONS
Mankato, MN

CRESTWOOD HOUSE
Mankato, Minnesota

LIBRARY OF CONGRESS CATALOGING IN PUBLICATION DATA
Green, Carl R.
  The giraffe.

  (Wildlife, habits & habitat)
  SUMMARY: Examines the appearance, behavior, and life cycle of the giraffe and describes modern efforts to protect it.
  1. Giraffes--Juvenile literature. (1. Giraffes) I. Sanford, William R. (William Reynolds). II. Schroeder, Howard. III. Title. IV. Series.
  QL737.U56S26   1987   599.73'57   87-1363
  ISBN 0-89686-332-8

International Standard Book Number:	Library of Congress Catalog Card Number:
Library Binding 0-89686-332-8	87-1363

ILLUSTRATION CREDITS:

Cover Photo: Nadine Orabona/Stock Concepts
Stephen J. Krasemann/DRK Photo: 5, 8, 36
Jim Brandenburg/DRK Photo: 6
Leonard Lee Rue III: 11, 19, 27
Lynn M. Stone: 12, 15, 35
Rod Allin/Tom Stack & Associates: 20
Leonard Rue Jr.: 23
Erwin & Peggy Bauer: 24-25, 28, 32, 45
Nadine Orabona/Stock Concepts: 31, 39, 43
Joseph Berke: 40
Bob Williams: 46

Copyright© 1987 by Crestwood House, Inc. All rights reserved. No part of this book may be reproduced in any form without written permission from the publisher, except for brief passages included in a review. Printed in the United States of America.

Hwy. 66 South, Box 3427
Mankato, MN 56002-3427

TABLE OF CONTENTS

Introduction: The animal with the long neck 4
Chapter One: The giraffe in close-up 9
   Finding a proper name
   The tallest animal on earth
   Many horns and a well-adapted body
   A vegetarian with four stomachs
   Giraffes depend on their eyes and ears
   More vocal than people think
Chapter Two: The giraffe in its African habitat 17
   A peaceful, social animal
   A leafy diet
   Drinking can be awkward
   Faster than they look
   Sleep and rest
   Enemies come in all sizes
   Few giraffes die of old age
Chapter Three: The life cycle of the giraffe 26
   A six-foot baby
   A group of playful calves
   A visit to the water hole
   A close call
   A curious young giraffe
   The cycle is complete
Chapter Four: Can the world's tallest animal survive? ... 34
   Hunted as well as loved
   Giraffes are real
   Human predators
   Is the giraffe endangered?
   What are giraffes good for?
Chapter Five: Saving the Rothschild giraffe 40
   A plan to save the Rothschild
   A long chase
   The danger isn't over
   A friend for Daisy
   Friends, not pets
Map 46
Index/Glossary 47

INTRODUCTION:

The open-sided safari bus creaked and bounced across Kenya's Nairobi National Park. Sara Finch, the safari guide, pointed out a rhinoceros to the tourists. Old Mr. Power was so excited that he shot an entire roll of film in less than a minute.

Morgan O'Connor carefully clicked off three pictures. "Kelsie, did you see Mr. Power? He used an entire roll of film," he whispered to his sister. "I'm saving most of mine. Sara said we'd see some giraffes today."

Ten minutes later, Kelsie spotted five tall, slender animals near some thorny trees. "There they are!" she called. "Giraffes!"

The driver steered the bus close to the animals. The giraffes stared down at the visitors and then continued to feed. Morgan focused his camera on a big male's leaf-shaped brown spots. "That giraffe must be twenty feet tall!" he gasped.

Sara heard him. "No, he's only about sixteen feet tall, and half of that is neck," she laughed. "As you can see, the giraffes use their long necks to reach the tender leaves at the top of these acacia trees. Other leaf-eating animals can't reach that high, so giraffes don't have to compete for food."

Kelsie tried to imagine an X-ray of a giraffe's neck.

A giraffe uses its long neck to reach the leaves on an acacia tree.

"They must have a lot of bones in those long necks," she said.

"Giraffes are full of surprises," Sara told her. "Humans, mice, and giraffes all have seven major bones in their necks. The difference is that a giraffe's vertebrae are over a foot long. Tough bands of tissue hold the bones together."

"Sara, is it true that giraffes can't bend down far enough to touch the ground with their heads?" Mr. Power asked.

"That's only a myth," Sara replied. "How else would a giraffe get a drink? They spread their legs apart

The giraffe needs to spread its legs apart to be able to drink water.

and bend their necks. Sometimes they also bend their knees. They don't like to keep their heads down, because it makes them dizzy."

"A dizzy giraffe! That sounds as bad as a giraffe with a sore throat," Morgan said.

"You'd get dizzy, too, if the blood pressure in your brain doubled when you put your head down," Sara laughed. "Controlling the flow of blood in a six-foot neck is a big problem. The main neck artery has muscles that help the heart pump the blood upward. Also, the vein that carries blood away from the brain has valves to keep the blood from flowing the wrong way. Even so, blood pressure can build up and make the animal dizzy."

The driver started the engine. "Any more questions?" Sara asked. "We have to reach the water hole before noon."

"Have giraffes always had long necks?" Kelsie wondered.

"No one knows for sure," Sara replied. "One theory suggests that nature favored the giraffes with the longest necks. Unable to compete for food, the short-necked giraffes died out."

Sara paused while the bus bounced across a stream. "My favorite myth comes from African storytellers," she added. "They say that God decided to make one last animal. He started with some leftover parts from the camel and the leopard. But He still wasn't satisfied.

The giraffe is a graceful animal. Its grace is especially noticed when it is running.

So He stretched and stretched the creature's neck and legs. The result was the giraffe!''

Morgan looked back. Something had scared the giraffes, and the herd was galloping away. Their long, graceful strides carried them across the plain with surprising speed. ''I won't argue with that story,'' he said. ''The giraffe is certainly Africa's tallest creature—and one of its most beautiful.''

CHAPTER ONE:

Ancient naturalists had a hard time classifying the giraffe. The Greeks thought the tall, graceful animal was a cross between a camel and a leopard. An Arab wise man disagreed. He claimed that giraffes resulted from a two-step process. First, a hyena mated with a camel. Then the hyena-camel produced a giraffe by mating with a wild cow!

Finding a proper name

The naturalists of the 1700's, who classified the giraffe, ignored these old myths. The first step was easy. Giraffes are mammals—warm-blooded animals that give birth to live young. Next, they found that giraffes have an even number of "toes" inside each hoof. That fact put them in the group *Artiodactyla,* along with deer and camels.

The next step was harder. At first, the naturalists put giraffes in the same family as elk and deer. When they realized that giraffes didn't fit there, they moved them into a family of their own, the *Giraffidae.* (The much smaller okapi is the only other member of this family.) Finally, they gave giraffes a species name. Someone must have remembered the myth about the camel and the leopard. To this day, scientists know the giraffe as *Giraffa camelopardalis*.

At least twelve subspecies of *Giraffa camelopardalis* still live in Africa. The varieties differ only in color, markings, and the number of horns. Each subspecies developed when a breeding population lived apart from other giraffes for many years. The most common subspecies of the giraffe are the reticulated, Nubian, Masai, Rothschild, Zambian, and Cape.

Even experts have to look carefully to tell one subspecies from another. All giraffes have coats of short, stiff hair and stubby manes that run down the back of their necks. Each subspecies, however, has its own color and spots. Reticulated giraffes have regular, dark brown spots separated by fine tan lines. Masai giraffes, in contrast, wear jagged spots separated by wide, uneven tan areas. A third variety, the Cape giraffe, has blotchy spots with dark centers and lighter edges. The number of horns also varies. Northern giraffes have three to five horns, but the southern varieties have only two.

The tallest animal on earth

The giraffe is the world's tallest animal. Measured at the shoulder, adult males (called bulls) may stand ten to twelve feet (3 to 3.7 m) tall. Their necks add

The giraffe is the world's tallest animal. They can be up to eighteen feet (5.5 m) tall.

another six feet (1.8 m), for a total height of fifteen to eighteen feet (4.6 to 5.5 m)! Cows (females) average a foot (30 cm) shorter than the bulls. Although they look delicate, giraffes aren't lightweights. An adult bull weighs 2,600 to 3,000 pounds (1,180 to 1,362 kg). The cows are about five hundred pounds (227 kg) lighter.

Naturalists have long wondered about the giraffe's unusual body shape. The animal's height allows it to reach the food it needs, but is that its only value? One theory states that being tall and slender helps get rid of extra body heat. In a hot climate, that's important. Heavy animals, such as the hippopotamus, must keep cool by wallowing in mud and water. Giraffes, by contrast, don't seem to mind the direct sun. Only on the hottest days do they look for shade.

On very hot days, giraffes like a place that is shaded from the sun.

Many horns and a well-adapted body

Perched at the end of its long neck, a giraffe's head has a slightly camel-like shape. The snout is more pointed, however, and unlike camels, giraffes have horns. All giraffes have at least two twelve-inch (30 cm) horns. Each knobby horn is covered with skin and hair. The northern varieties have a large bump in the center of the forehead, which some people call a third horn. The Rothschild giraffe adds another pair of horn bumps behind the ears—a total of five "horns"!

The giraffe's body is adapted to its unusual size and shape. To fill its long neck and windpipe, the giraffe breathes in three times as much air as a buffalo. To pump blood to its big body, its heart is five times larger than a human heart. Unlike most big animals, giraffes have a rapid heart rate—about 150 beats per minute. Giraffes also appear to be the smartest of all hoofed animals.

Compared to its neck and long legs, the giraffe has a rather short body. The front legs are longer than the back legs. This causes the spine to slope downward toward the tail. The length from the base of the neck to the beginning of the tail is about five feet (1.5 m). This shape makes it easier for the giraffe to balance its long, heavy neck. The slender legs look fragile, but they're very strong. Each leg ends in a horny hoof similar to a horse's hoof. The hoof is split into two parts, and each part is the hardened tip of one toe. The tail is about three feet (1 m) long, with a tuft of long black hair at the end.

A vegetarian with four stomachs

The giraffe is a cud-chewing animal—in other words, a ruminant. Like other ruminants, giraffes have biting teeth only in their lower jaw. These teeth clip off leaves by biting against a hard pad in the upper jaw. Strong, flat molars line the sides of both jaws. The molars grind and crush the giraffe's diet of leaves, twigs, bark, and vines.

Digestion starts when partly chewed food passes into the first of the giraffe's four stomachs. Later, the giraffe brings half-digested balls of food (called cud) back from the second stomach for more chewing. On the average, a giraffe spends three to five hours a day ruminating (chewing its cud). It uses its molars to grind the tennis-ball-sized cud to a pulpy mush. When it's fully chewed, the giraffe again swallows the mush. More digestion takes place in the last two stomachs.

Giraffes have long, purple tongues. Eighteen inches (46 cm) in length, the tongue is covered with tough,

The tongue of the giraffe is long, strong, and rough.

raspy skin. An old African story says that calves run from their mothers to avoid being licked with their raspy tongues. That's a myth, but the tough surface does have a purpose. It allows the giraffe to feed on thorny trees that other animals won't touch.

Giraffes depend on their eyes and ears

The giraffe constantly watches for danger. From its towering height, its sharp eyes can spot a predator a mile away. Zebras and other grazing animals often feed near giraffes so they can share this early warning system. The giraffe's large eyes also have good color vision.

The giraffe's sense of hearing is sharper than its sense of smell. Each long ear rotates separately, so nothing escapes its notice. Even the slightest sound alerts the animal to danger. With such good eyes and ears, the giraffe uses its nose mostly for finding a mate. When necessary, it can close its narrow nostrils to keep out sand, dust, and water.

More vocal than people think

For many years, giraffes were thought to be voiceless. It's true that they aren't noisy, but neither are they mute. Their long throats have vocal cords that make several sounds. Young giraffes, for example, make a bleating noise when they're lonely. Bulls will snort and grunt loudly if they're angry or hungry. For their part, cows sometimes make a soft mooing sound.

In addition to sounds, giraffes "talk" to each other through body movements. The strongest bull in a herd holds his head higher than the other bulls. The switch of a tail or a sudden lowering of the neck also signals danger. Alertness is important, for the giraffe's habitat is full of predators.

CHAPTER TWO:

Thousands of years ago, the first true giraffes roamed the plains of central Asia. After reaching Africa, they died out in Asia. Today's giraffes live mainly in east-central and southern Africa. They prefer the tree-dotted grasslands, known as savannahs, for their habitat. These dry plains provide the trees and bush that giraffes eat.

A peaceful, social animal

Giraffes seem to enjoy one another's company. Seventy giraffes have been seen in a single herd, but that's unusual. Within a territory of twenty-five square miles (65 sq. km), giraffes tend to browse in small herds of five to seven. These small herds ignore one another, except during courtship and mating. A typical herd is made up of an older bull, several cows, and their calves. It's not uncommon, however, to see herds made up of all bulls, or all cows.

Within the herd, giraffes set up their own social order. The largest bull usually serves as herdmaster. If other bulls join the herd, the herdmaster quickly lets them know who's boss. Like people, some giraffes are bold and curious. Others are shy and timid. A wise old cow sometimes leads the herd as it browses.

A leafy diet

More than eighty-five percent of a giraffe's diet is made up of tree leaves. Other foods include shrubs and vines, bark, seed pods, and fruit. One favorite, the whistling thorn, also shelters nests of stinging ants. Neither thorns nor ants bother the giraffe, who easily spits them out. Grasses and herbs make up only one percent of the diet.

Adult giraffes eat nearly forty pounds (18 kg) of leaves a day. They browse from the tops of the trees down to about four feet (1.2 m) above the ground. After a herd has fed, the trees look as though a gardener has been pruning and shaping them. Giraffes sniff their food before feeding, but sight seems to be more important than smell. In a London zoo, a giraffe used to snatch fake fruit from the hats of women visitors!

Drinking can be awkward

When water holes are full, giraffes tend to drink water every day. Captive giraffes, for example, drink about two gallons (7.6 liters) of water a day. During periods of drought, they get much of their water from their food. Acacia leaves, for example, are as much as three-fourths water. This allows the herds to search for food far from the nearest water hole.

Giraffes approach water holes with great caution, and always in groups. Bending down to drink is awkward, and leaves them open to attack by predators. At the water hole, the giraffe spreads its front legs apart before lowering its head. Sometimes it also bends its knees in order to reach the water. Even when it's drinking, the giraffe stays alert. It raises its head every minute or two to check for danger.

Giraffes are always on the alert for danger, especially at a water hole.

19

Faster than they look

People who see giraffes for the first time expect them to be awkward and slow. However, these tall, graceful animals can outrun a horse for a short distance! They can also jump fences and bushes with ease.

Giraffes have three gaits: the walk, the pace, and the gallop. A browsing giraffe walks slowly, moving one leg at a time. This gives it a three-legged support at all times. To move faster, it changes to a pacing walk. When pacing, a giraffe moves both right legs forward,

A giraffe can run faster than a horse over a short distance.

then its left legs. As its speed increases, the giraffe's neck pumps up and down. Pacing moves the giraffe along at ten miles (16 km) per hour.

To escape danger, giraffes shift into a high-speed gallop. First, the giraffe pushes off with its hind legs as its neck arches forward. Its front legs strike and push off as the hind legs come forward—ahead of the forelegs—and the neck moves back. This rocking-horse neck movement helps the giraffe keep its balance. Each stride covers ten feet (3 m) or more. At full speed, giraffes have been clocked running at thirty-five miles (56 km) per hour. A galloping giraffe curls its tail over its back to keep it from catching in the thorn bushes.

Sleep and rest

Giraffes rest often, but sleep very little. They usually feed in early morning, early evening, and after midnight. During the hot midday hours, they rest and chew their cud. Some giraffes stand while resting, but others lie down. The giraffe usually holds its neck erect while lying down, but it sometimes rests it on a hip or a low tree limb. A nap rarely lasts longer than four minutes. Getting up is awkward. The giraffe must thrust its neck forward and back several times to help it scramble to its feet.

Rest periods also give giraffes time for grooming. The animals lick their short coats and bite at itchy spots.

If its underbelly itches, a giraffe may rub against a thorn bush. Oxpeckers also help rid the animal of ticks and flies. These birds make a meal of the pests that live on the giraffe's skin.

Enemies come in all sizes

The giraffe's size and strength protect it from most predators. Leopards, crocodiles, hyenas and pythons will attack a calf or an old, lame adult. But only lions regularly hunt full-grown giraffes. The herds seem to know that lions are deadly enemies. They gallop off as soon as they spot a stalking lion.

Insect pests, parasites, and diseases also threaten the giraffe. Tapeworms, ticks, and flies live in and on the animal's body. A cattle disease called rinderpest, which reached Africa in the 1890's, also kills many giraffes. In 1960, for example, rinderpest wiped out forty percent of the giraffes in northern Kenya.

Slow-healing wounds are also a problem. Flies often lay eggs in the deep claw marks left by a lion. The hatching maggots attract oxpeckers, which peck at the sores.

Few giraffes die of old age

In the wild, many calves die in the first few months. If they survive the first year, they may live to be twenty years old or more. As with other wild animals, few giraffes die of old age. When they grow old and weak, predators pull them down. Death is a necessary part of nature's life cycle.

In the wild, a giraffe can live up to twenty years.

The giraffe's life cycle is filled with dangers, and only the most physically fit survive.

CHAPTER THREE:

A naturalist lies hidden in a clump of high grass. She studies the small herd of Masai giraffes with her night glasses. The tall animals look ghostly against the pale November sky. As the scientist watches, she scribbles notes on a pad. The cow she calls Twiggy is calving.

A six-foot baby

A hundred yards away, Twiggy waits for her calf to be born. She mated fifteen months ago with a bull. Six other giraffes stand nearby, ready to defend the newborn calf. The scent of lions is heavy in the air.

The calf is born headfirst and drops to the ground. The five-foot (1.5 m) fall breaks the umbilical cord that connects it to the cow. The shock also starts the newborn's breathing. Twiggy turns and licks the calf with her rough tongue. The naturalist has time to see that it's a female calf. Then the other giraffes cut off her view.

"I'll call the calf Sunny," she tells herself. "If she's like most calves, she's about six feet (1.8 m) tall and weighs 140 pounds (64 kg). Under the skin of her head, her knobby little horns were pushed over during the birth process. In a few weeks they'll stand up and

This three-day-old Masai giraffe is already about six feet (1.8 m) tall.

connect solidly to the bones of the skull. I could see that Sunny's jagged spots are a pale brown. They'll turn darker as she grows up."

Within the hour, the naturalist sees Sunny nursing at one of her mother's four teats. "She'll grow fast," she writes. "The milk has five times more protein than a dairy cow's milk."

A group of playful calves

For the first few days, Twiggy nudges the calf back between her legs when Sunny tries to wander. After Sunny learns her mother's scent, she follows in Twiggy's shadow as the herd moves from tree to tree.

Families of giraffes move together in herds from one feeding area to another.

At two or three weeks, Sunny adds acacia leaves to her diet. She still runs to nurse several times a day, however. Twiggy won't wean her until Sunny is at least nine months old.

Twiggy sometimes leaves Sunny in the care of another cow. This "auntie" often has two or three calves in her care. The calves seem to enjoy the change. They gallop in circles and kick up their heels. Sometimes they put on a mock battle by swinging their heads and necks against each other. The thick bones of their skulls absorb the shock without injury.

A visit to the water hole

Every few days, the herd visits the water hole. The giraffes move slowly, watching and listening for danger. When they reach the water hole, Sunny stays well back from the soft edge. Instinct tells her that giraffes can get stuck in the mud. Like other giraffes, the calf doesn't know how to swim—and will never learn. Sunny's long legs wobble and bend as she leans down to the water. Twice she has to rear back and regain her balance. At last, she manages to take a long drink.

Nearby, two young bulls start a sparring contest. Standing stiff-legged, one bull swings his neck at his opponent. The second bull dodges and then swings back. Their strong necks whack against each other with great force. The bulls also jab with their horns. This battle is just for fun, but a serious fight, which involves kicking with sharp hoofs, can leave one of the bulls dead or badly wounded. In a serious fight, the powerful whacks of the necks can be heard at a distance of one hundred yards (91 m).

When the battle is over, Sunny misses her mother. She finds Twiggy licking a large rock. Sunny sticks out her tongue and tastes salt. The flavor of the "salt lick" rock is delicious!

A close call

That night, Twiggy lies down in the grass to rest. Sunny sleeps with her head resting on Twiggy's back. An hour later, a pack of hyenas attacks the herd. The hyenas are hoping to snatch Sunny away before the adult giraffes can react.

A watchful bull quickly steps between Sunny and the hyenas. With one powerful swing of his neck, he sends the lead hyena flying. Another hyena tries to slip past, but the bull breaks its back with a well-aimed kick. By then, Twiggy and Sunny are on their feet. As they gallop off, the other giraffes follow them. The hyenas give up the chase a few minutes later.

When the giraffes stop to chew their cud, they stay on their feet. The hyenas are gone, but the breeze carries the sharp scent of lions. A few miles away, the great predators bring down an old male giraffe. One lioness holds the bull's attention while another leaps on him from behind. But Sunny has been lucky. More than fifty percent of all calves die during the first year.

A curious young giraffe

Sunny spends much of her first year in a giraffe "nursery school." Two old cows stay with the calves while their mothers feed some distance away. Family ties are loose in a giraffe herd. One calf wanders away from its mother and is adopted by another cow. By now, Sunny has grown to ten feet (3 m) in height. She no longer nurses from Twiggy's teats.

A young giraffe nurses from its mother at the San Diego Zoo in California.

Like most calves, Sunny is curious about everything. She sniffs at warthogs, lizards, and snakes. A stork backs away from Sunny's curious snout and squawks angrily. When Sunny doesn't back off, the stork pecks her on the nose. Sunny bleats loudly and gallops back to Twiggy.

At eighteen months, the calves begin to leave their mothers. The males wander off to form a herd of their own. Later, they'll split up and fight for places in mixed herds. Some of the females stay with Twiggy's herd,

After eighteen months, a female calf is allowed to join a herd.

but Sunny goes off on her own. A giant bull named Miti allows her to join his herd.

The cycle is complete

At three years of age, Sunny is fully grown. Only her bony skull is still growing—new bone will be added all through her life. Like other cows, Sunny comes into heat every twelve to fifteen days. This allows her to mate at any time during the year.

Miti begins the courtship dance. He stands next to her, and rubs his neck against hers. Then he licks her tail. Sunny moves away, but Miti follows her. When she urinates, he tastes the liquid for the chemicals that tell him she's ready to mate. The two giraffes mate several times during the next three hours.

The naturalist returns to study Sunny. She knows that illegal hunters have been shooting giraffes in the game park. "The giraffe has survived all its other enemies," she writes in her notebook. "Can it survive contact with human beings?"

CHAPTER FOUR:

Almost everyone who sees a giraffe falls head-over-heels in love with it. Perhaps it's the animal's grace, its height, or its beautiful hide. Whatever the reason, the love affair has been going on for a long time. The word "giraffe" probably comes from "zarafa," an old Arabic word that means "creature of grace" or "one who walks swiftly."

Hunted as well as loved

Stone Age African tribes worshipped the giraffe, but they also hunted it. The meat could be eaten, and the hide made a good, tough leather. Killing a giraffe must have been difficult, however. Hunters couldn't always catch the fast, alert giraffes, and stone arrowheads bounced off their inch-thick (2.5 cm) hides. These early hunters painted pictures of giraffes on their cave walls. Two thousand years later, the Egyptians decorated pottery with their own drawings of giraffes.

Stories about the giraffe reached the Greeks from Egypt. Having never seen a giraffe, the early Greeks called it the "leopard-spotted camel." Europeans finally saw the real thing about 46 B.C. That's when Julius Caesar paraded a giraffe through Rome. Some historians think the animal was a gift from the famous Queen Cleopatra of Egypt.

Giraffes are real

During the Middle Ages, most people thought the giraffe was a myth, like the unicorn. A few European rulers did keep giraffes in their private zoos. Even so, the drawings in books of "Cameliopardus" (a Roman word) were wildly inaccurate.

In the early 1800's, zoos in Austria, France, and England each received a giraffe. After people saw these "mythical" animals, no one could doubt that they existed. The British and Austrian giraffes died, but the French giraffe lived for sixteen years. The first giraffe

Giraffes were first put into zoos in the early 1800's.

arrived in the United States in 1837. Forty years later, the Philadelphia Zoo's herd had grown to include five bulls and a cow.

Human predators

While city people were first seeing giraffes in zoos, native hunters were killing wild giraffes. Armed with rifles, the hunters found it easy to bring down the great animals. The natives ate the meat and tanned the hide to make buckets, shields, drums, and whips. The long, black tail hair was made into fly whisks. Witch doctors also used the hair in their charms. Today, poachers still

In the past, the natives of Africa had many uses for the giraffe.

cut the tail hair to make into woven bracelets. They sell the bracelets to tourists.

For the Arabs of the Sudan, hunting giraffes was once a test of skill and courage. Only the fastest horses could catch a galloping giraffe. Once alongside the giraffe, the rider tried to cut the animal's leg muscles with a sword. This was a risky sport. A panicky animal sometimes killed a rider with one swing of its neck or a single swift kick. Because of this danger, a hunter who killed as many as fifteen giraffes was highly honored for his bravery and skill.

Is the giraffe endangered?

At one time, giraffes ranged over great areas of what now are Kenya, Tanzania, Somalia, and South Africa. No one thought the giraffes would ever disappear. They browsed on land that people don't usually farm—dry grasslands dotted with trees and thornbush.

As this century began, settlers moved into the African wilderness. Each new farm and village reduced the size of the giraffe's habitat. Poor farmers hunted them for their hides, and settlers wiped out the giraffe in the Kalahari Desert. Big-game hunters took thousands more as trophies.

After World War II, the African nations set aside wildland habitat for endangered animals. As a result, game parks in Kenya, Tanzania, and the Republic of South Africa now support large herds of giraffes. Game wardens guard the animals from poachers, who would kill a giraffe just to take its tail. The United States and other countries help by refusing to import products made from giraffe hides. This makes poaching less profitable.

Despite this protection, giraffes are still in danger. Growing human populations need more and more land. As farms move into wildlife habitat, governments allow farmers to shoot giraffes that are destroying their crops. A few big-game hunters also buy licenses to shoot giraffes. Telephone lines are another problem. Giraffes are so tall that their necks get tangled in the wires!

What are giraffes good for?

All the efforts to turn giraffes into farm animals have failed. It's just as well. No one can ride on a giraffe's slanted back, nor can a sixteen-foot (4.9 m) animal be harnessed to pull a plow. Only the animals' meat and hides are useful, and domestic cattle provide these products more cheaply.

Even though giraffes can't be tamed, the animal does well in captivity. Once captured, giraffes soon lose their fear of humans. Tourists who drive through wild-animal parks love to see giraffes looking down at them. For their part, the giraffes sometimes lick the tops of the

Giraffes will sometimes lick the tops of cars as tourists drive through wild-animal parks.

cars and buses. They seem to prefer yellow vehicles.

Naturalists argue that giraffes are worth saving simply because they exist. The sight of these tall, stately creatures fills us with a sense of nature's wild beauty. Maybe that's why people are working so hard to save this endangered species.

CHAPTER FIVE:

Betty and Jock Leslie-Melville often have guests for breakfast at their estate near Nairobi, Kenya. Most of their guests are human. But their favorite guest is a Rothschild giraffe named Daisy.

Visitors just about jump out of their chairs when Daisy appears. She sticks her long neck through the window and waits until Betty gives her a waffle. Daisy seems to enjoy the snack. Before she leaves, she rewards Betty with a giraffe kiss.

A giraffe can be very affectionate, even with people.

A plan to save the Rothschild

Daisy's story started when Kenya opened some new land to farming. That was good news for the farmers, but bad news for the Rothschild giraffe. Naturalists knew that the new settlers would kill any giraffes that broke their fences or ate their crops. To make it worse, the last 180 Rothschild giraffes in Kenya lived in that area. The naturalists believed that the beautiful subspecies would be extinct in a few years.

Betty and Jock worked out a simple plan to save the Rothschild giraffes from extinction. They decided to capture a pair of calves and raise them on their estate. Although the plan was simple, they knew it wouldn't be easy. Their work as safari guides had taught them to respect the size and strength of the giraffe.

A friend named Jock Rutherfurd said he'd catch the giraffes for them. Rutherfurd's plan was to rope the calves! After his horse cut a calf off from its mother, he'd slip a rope loop over the young one's head. Betty and Jock would follow in a van, ready to take the calf back to its new home.

A long chase

When they reached the herd, Rutherfurd cut a calf loose, as planned. But he hadn't counted on the chase that followed. The young female galloped off, with Rutherfurd right behind. The calf ran for three miles before Rutherfurd could rope her. Then he had to wrestle the kicking calf to the ground. After he blindfolded her with his shirt, she calmed down a little.

When the van arrived, the Leslie-Melvilles still had a problem. How do you put an eight-foot (2.4 m), 450-pound (204 kg) giraffe where it doesn't want to go? Finally, they managed to shove the struggling calf into the van. Even then, someone had to ride with her. If her head stayed down too long, she might die from the buildup of blood pressure in her brain.

The danger isn't over

Betty and Jock were already calling the calf Daisy. They put her into a special stall with its own corral. The danger wasn't over. Daisy might die from the shock of the chase and capture. If she lived through the first night, she still had only a fifty-fifty chance of living through the next two days.

Everyone cheered when Daisy drank some milk on the second day. When the calf finished, she bent down and kissed Jock with her rubbery lips. Two days later, she was eating the yellow flowers from an acacia tree. The crisis was over.

From that time on, Daisy seemed to think of Jock

as her mother. He fed her panfuls of milk mixed with cod-liver oil. She was a messy eater. As Daisy slurped the milk, it splashed in all directions. Within a week, she was eating carrots from peoples' hands. Betty and Jock began to plan for the future.

A friend for Daisy

A few weeks later, the team captured a male calf. Daisy ignored Marlon at first. A few days later, she started acting like his mother. Betty guessed that Daisy took the job because there weren't any adult giraffes around. With Daisy to calm him, Marlon quickly

This Rothschild cow and calf were photographed at the San Diego Zoo in California.

adjusted to captivity. When the calves were ready, the Leslie-Melvilles turned them loose on the estate. Despite their freedom, the young giraffes never tried to run away.

Daisy and Marlon grew rapidly, as much as an eighth of an inch (32 mm) a day. (If that doesn't sound like much, imagine a school friend who grows ten inches (25 cm) during the summer!) After the first year, giraffes stopped drinking milk. They browsed on the estate's many trees.

When they weren't eating, the two giraffes played games. One favorite game was tag. If Marlon was "it," he chased Daisy in giant figure-eights for several minutes. After a brief rest, they changed places and started again. Sometimes they varied the game by crashing into each other. The young giraffes also learned to dance! When they heard music on the radio, they swayed to the beat. Visitors thought they looked like giant ballet dancers.

Friends, not pets

The giraffes showed a great deal of love toward Betty and Jock. They nuzzled, kissed, and licked their human friends. Sometimes they sucked on Betty's thumb. But Daisy and Marlon weren't tame, nor were they pets. There was always a hint of wildness in their behavior. Even so, the giraffes were sensitive to human feelings.

They seemed to know which visitors feared or disliked animals. They stayed away from those people.

Betty and Jock say their tall, graceful friends have given them much pleasure. But they never forget that their aim is to save the Rothschild giraffe. They're looking forward to the day when Daisy and Marlon will mate. In time, these two giraffes may start a whole new herd.

Like other people who love the giraffe, the Leslie-Melvilles have a dream. They hope for a future in which no child will ever have to ask, "What did the giraffe look like?"

Hopefully, this peaceful African scene will be repeated for years to come.

MAP:

AFRICA

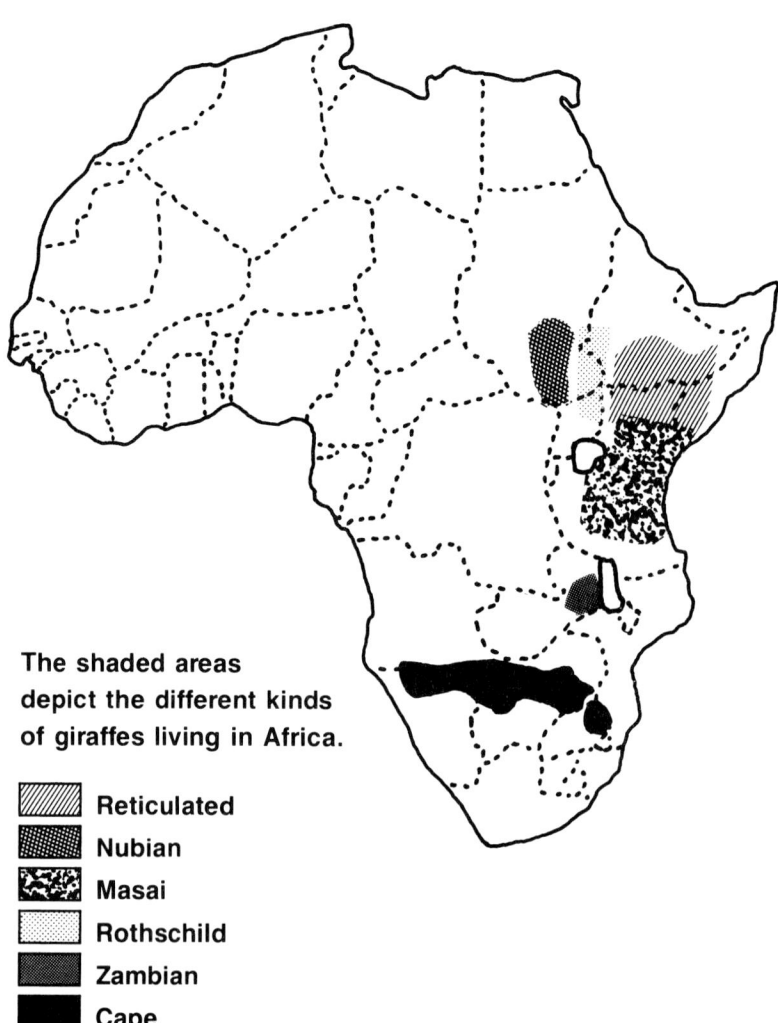

The shaded areas depict the different kinds of giraffes living in Africa.

- Reticulated
- Nubian
- Masai
- Rothschild
- Zambian
- Cape

INDEX/GLOSSARY:

BROWSING ANIMAL 17, 18, 20, 37, 44 — *An animal that eats twigs, bark, leaves, vines, and other plants that grow above ground level.*

BULL 12, 16, 17, 26, 29, 30, 33, 36 — *An adult male giraffe.*

CALF 17, 22, 26, 28, 29, 31, 32, 41, 42, 43, 44 — *A young male or female giraffe.*

COW 12, 16, 17, 26, 28, 29, 31, 33, 36, 43 — *An adult female giraffe.*

CUD 14, 21, 30 — *Partly digested food that a giraffe brings up from its second stomach to be chewed into a pulpy mush.*

DROUGHT 18 — *A long period of time without rain.*

ENDANGERED SPECIES 37, 39 — *An animal that is in danger of becoming extinct.*

EXTINCT 41 — *When the last member of a species dies.*

GROOMING 21 — *An animal's way of cleaning itself. Giraffes groom by licking and biting at their bodies.*

HABITAT 16, 17, 37, 38 — *The place where an animal makes its home.*

HEAT 33 — *The time during which a female animal mates and can become pregnant.*

MUTE 16 — *A voiceless animal; one that can't make a sound.*

MYTH 6, 7, 9, 10, 15, 35 — *A story that many people believe but which is almost always untrue.*

NATURALIST 9, 12, 26, 28, 33, 39, 41 — *A scientist who studies plants and animals.*

POACHERS 33, 36, 38 — *Hunters who kill animals illegally.*

PREDATOR 15, 16, 19, 22, 23, 30, 36 — *An animal that lives by hunting and killing other animals.*

RINDERPEST 22 — *A viral disease that kills many kinds of grazing and browsing animals.*

RUMINANT 14 — *An animal that chews its cud while it rests.*

SAVANNAH 17 — *A flat, nearly treeless African grassland.*

SUBSPECIES 10, 41 — *Closely related varieties of a single animal species.*

TEATS 28, 31 — *The nipples of a cow giraffe. Calves suck on the teats to obtain milk.*

READ AND ENJOY THE SERIES:

If you would like to know more about all kinds of wildlife, you should take a look at the other books in this series.

You'll find books on bald eagles and other birds. Books on alligators and other reptiles. There are books about deer and other big-game animals. And there are books about sharks and other creatures that live in the ocean.

In all of the books you will learn that life in the wild is not easy. But you will also learn what people can do to help wildlife survive. So read on!